Collecting Paper Money as an Investment

by
Irwin Tyler

Ahl Kayn Publishing

Spring Valley, New York

Collecting Paper Money with Confidence

ISBN 978-1-304-63235-7
© Copyright 2013, by
Irwin Tyler
Ahl Kayn Publications

Spring Valley, New York

ALL RIGHTS RESERVED
INCLUDING THE RIGHTS OF REPRODUCTION
IN WHOLE OR IN PART IN ANY FORM

First Printing - **2013**

Manufactured in the United States of America

TABLE OF CONTENTS

4 PAPER CURRENCY – COLLECTING WITH CONFIDENCE
  5 PAPER
  6 INK
  6 ENGRAVING
  6 NATURE OF PAPER CURRENCY
    8 CRISPNESS
    9 STAINING
    9 SOILING
    10 PINCHES
    10 CREASES
    12 SPLITS
    12 SKEWED DESIGN
    13 SHIFTED DESIGN
    14 ABNORMAL MARGINS
    15 CLARITY
    16 SPLATTERS
    17 DISCOLORATION
    17 FOXING
    18 ROUNDED CORNERS
    18 INK MIGRATION
    19 INK FADING
    20 PERFORATIONS
    21 HOLES
    22 CLIPPING
    23 TRIM
    24 ROUGHNESS
    25 WEAR
    26 INK BREAK
    26 THIN SPOTS
    27 SURFACE DEFECTS
    29 IMBEDDED MATTER
    30 WRINKLES
  30 OTHER FACTORS AFFECTING GRADING
32 REFERENCES
35 OTHER PUBLICATIONS BY IRWIN TYLER

PAPER CURRENCY – COLLECTING WITH CONFIDENCE

If you have ever felt unsure about the grade of a note in your hand, and just what price to put on it, you are not alone. Most collectors and dealers gain confidence in their ability to grade and value a note through years of sometimes costly experience. The more you know about paper currency the more confident you will feel grading your notes, and in negotiating a fair price.. This book will help you to dramatically shorten the time it takes you to become a confident, accurate and consistent grader of paper currency. So, let's begin.

Paper money had its origins in China in the 14th Century as an alternative to metal coins. The need for metal in the economy was deemed more necessary than metal's use for coinage. This led to the creation of paper currency and, eventually, to its collection.

Various factors determine the nature, grade, and quality of paper currency. These include the nature and amount of material making up the paper, the manufacturing process used, the chemicals and sizing (a glue-like substance) added, and the roller pressure applied. Drying conditions and drying speed are additional influences.

Other factors contributing to the quality of paper currency include the quality of the ink used, the complexity and quality of the engravings, the plate material (wood block, steel plate, etc.), and the printing itself (intaglio, lithograph, etc. and the inspection process).

Great variability may thus be found in the same note produced at different times or different places.

PAPER

Many kinds of paper have been used for notes (and bonds, warrants, checks, etc.). Most note material is in reality a form of cloth. Heavy, coarse material was used to produce some of the earliest currency issues as well as the modern Concentration Camp notes. Some currencies, particularly state, municipal, and private issues, have been printed on other materials, as well. These include wood-based fibers. More's the pity for the delicate nature of these papers.

Modern United States currency paper is a standard for the highest quality. Most nations have adopted similarly high standards for their modern currencies. Such papers are crisp, heavyweight without being stiff, usually dull but smooth-surfaced. Newer materials, plastic and plasticized fibers among these, are now being tried in an attempt to prevent counterfeiting.

Older currencies, such as United States fractional notes of the mid-nineteenth century were produced on high-quality papers of a different type. Such papers often included thick colored threads as an anti-counterfeiting device. These threads frequently extended above the paper's surface, creating a bumpy texture.

Thinner papers were used to produce Confederate States of America (CSA) notes and notes of the southern states of that same period. Southern states notes also were produced on a variety of poorer-quality papers. With different papers shrinking at varying rates over time, southern states notes can now be found in varying sizes even though of the same type.

INK

Delicate, too, are the inks used for printing paper currency. Ink must resist fading and discoloration, wear, and the effects of temperature and humidity. The history of paper money includes patented inks "guaranteed" impossible to reproduce illegally.

ENGRAVING

High quality engraving, with its ability to reproduce fine details, is another factor in the development of paper money. The engraver's art has been a factor in establishing the legitimacy of paper money to the public and in minimizing counterfeiting of paper currency.

NATURE OF PAPER CURRENCY

Defects in paper currency are important, for they affect the grade and the consequent value collectors place on an item. Many conditions affect paper currency quality. The paper itself, inking, and the signatures and serial number stamping are subject to production defects. Other influences are the effects of storage and aging, and damage from handling (distribution and circulation).

A well-controlled production process using high-quality paper and ink is more likely to produce high quality notes. These are better able to survive the rigors of mishandling and the ravages of time.

Certain issues typically contain obvious production defects. One reason may be that better technologies were not available or were too costly. High production costs sometimes make stringent controls less likely. Too, poorly maintained production facilities will usually produce notes of poor quality. This may be unavoidable during wartime conditions, where volume is sometimes more important than quality.

Private issues and currencies issued during stressful economic conditions also are more likely to be issued with major defects. CSA and the German Notgeld issues are typical examples.

Certain issues have been more susceptible to damage from mishandling and aging. These include early issues of municipalities and other political subdivisions, and other issuers using lower-quality paper.

CRISPNESS

Crisp paper maintains a rigidity and has a solid feel. A crisp note will crackle audibly when shaken. Uncirculated notes and lightly circulated notes are crisp early in their lives. This changes rapidly with handling.

Handling introduces perspiration. Humidity and air-borne chemicals also enter into the paper. Add wrinkles and creases as the notes pass from hand to hand, and the note becomes more and more limp.

Different types of paper lose their crispness at different rates as they age. Lesser-grade papers are more easily affected by handling, losing crispness more quickly. Too, lesser-grade papers used for currency may be less crisp at the outset than high-quality papers.

In an attempt to upgrade a note, it may be starched. This usually can be detected by the somewhat "cardboard" feel of the note or by an unusually smooth and shiny surface. This artificial crispness may be "out of character" with other characteristics and defects discovered in the note.

STAINING

Stains are deposits on a note which pass into the paper itself. Staining is almost surely an indication of circulation. However, this is not an absolute, as water staining may have come from careless storage or storage accidents, not through normal circulation.

Stains come most often from liquid spills and from writing with a pen.

Stains are virtually impossible to remove. Water-based stains may be lightened, and possibly removed, by a cool water bath. The water does no harm to paper and printer's ink but will affect hand written signatures and serial numbers. Careful and controlled drying are necessary to maintain the prior condition of the paper and its surface.

Removing stains should not be undertaken lightly.

SOILING

Circulated notes often show soiling. Soiling is a deposit on the surface of a note.

Soiling typically includes fingerprints and pencil writing. It also includes surface dirt and grime typical of normal daily activities. Light soiling does sometimes occur to notes which are dropped or

otherwise mishandled during counting or shipping. Older notes sometimes show penciled marks used as counting controls by tellers. It would be highly unusual for a teller to have used a pen rather than a pencil to write a control count on
a note.

Light soiling SOMETIMES can be removed without leaving evidence of the cleaning operation. This should not be undertaken without thought and considerable care.

PINCHES

A pinch is a light fold which does not reach two edges of the note. Pinches most often are contained completely within the body of the note without reaching any edge.

A pinch usually results from difficulty in picking up the note from a flat surface. The cause most often is static electricity or moisture on the flat surface causing the note to "stick".

CREASES

If a fold passes from one edge of a note to any other edge it is called a crease. For the most part, notes become creased as a result of normal circulation.

Small-sized notes typically have a vertical crease through or near the center of the note. This is primarily the result of folding and storage in a normal-sized billfold or pocket.

Large-sized notes typically have two vertical creases at approximately each third-point because they do not fit easily into a normal-sized billfold or pocket. Horizontal folds at the midpoint are also common in large-sized notes.

Attempts are occasionally made to remove a crease in order to hide evidence of circulation. Close examination may reveal ink breaks tracing the path of the original fold.

Prior to reaching circulation, notes are counted. In the process of leafing through the stack minor diagonal creases at one or more corners may occur. Unless there is contrary evidence, such minor creases should not be considered circulation defects.

Storage in a billfold can cause a note to attain a curl without actually becoming creased. This defect can be removed easily without detection.

SPLITS

Longitudinal separations of the paper along a fold are considered splits rather than tears. There are two primary causes for splits. Fiber damage from continual folding for storage in a billfold or pocket eventually damages the fibers. They soon separate along the fold. Abrasion along a fold line as a result of normal circulation is the other primary cause.

When a split first becomes noticeable, it may seem to be a longitudinal thinning defect in the paper. The clue to its being the start of a split is its being positioned within a crease.

Splits are found most often at an edge or where two creases cross. In the area where creases cross, paper fibers may actually be lost. The result is an irregular hole rather than a split.

A split does not always separate as completely as a tear. The edges of splits are rough, with fibers usually extending across the space between the edges of the split.

SKEWED DESIGN

A skewed design is a design which is rotated with respect to the edges of the note. The four edges of the note will be at right angles to each other unless an edge trimming defect has also occurred. The Skewed Design Defect is not common.

A skewed design can occur during printing when the paper is misaligned in the press. It can also occur, similarly, when the sheet is being cut.

In high quality operations, such as those of the Bank of England, the U.S. Bureau of Engraving and Printing or the American Bank Note Company, this defect usually is trapped during inspection. When it does pass through it normally is barely noticeable.

Low-quality print operations are more likely to release obviously skewed notes.

SHIFTED DESIGN

Either mis-trimming or mis-printing can cause a note to be off-center. This defect can occur only during production as the notes are cut from the sheets.

The note itself normally will be full-sized, that is, within normal production tolerances. A note which appears shifted but which is slightly undersized may have been hand-trimmed to remove an edge

13

defect. Paper shrinkage, however, can also cause a note to become undersized.

High quality operations, such as those of the U.S. Bureau of Engraving and Printing or the American Bank Note Company, have produced few notes with significant shifting.

Low-quality operations are more likely to produce shifted designs. In some cases the border will have almost disappeared. This defect is common in issues of the Confederate States of America. Their notes were usually hand-trimmed, with significant variability in results. Here, many notes were released for circulation with obvious design shifts as well as variations in overall size.

ABNORMAL MARGINS

When notes are trimmed from their sheets, this step sometimes produces margins which are wider or narrower than standard. When a note is well-centered but has margins which are uniformly wide or uniformly narrow it is said to have abnormal margins.

Oversized margins can occur only during production as the notes are cut from the sheets. Undersized margins can be produced either this way or by hand trimming to remove an edge or corner defect. There is no positive way to detect this alteration other than knowing that such a defect has not been documented for this note. While such hand trimming may create a note whose dimensions are slightly smaller than production tolerances would allow, normal paper shrinkage can also produce a similar effect. If shrinkage is the cause, it can be detected by the matching shrinkage of the printed design itself as well as the margins.

Automated trimming operations, such as those of the U.S. Bureau of Engraving and Printing or the American Bank Note Company, rarely have produced notes with abnormal margins.

Use of scissors or a hand-operated cutting blade to trim notes from the sheets are more likely to produce abnormal margins. This defect is common in issues of the Confederate States of America.

CLARITY

A clarity defect in a note detracts from the normal look expected of notes of its type. Clarity defects are related to the amount of ink deposited on the plates and to the pressure applied by the press. Other printing defects, such as blank or unprinted areas, white spaces or "gutter" lines, or smearing are more rightly considered printing errors. These are collected and valued on a different basis from the notes considered here.

When a plate is lightly but uniformly inked or the pressure on the press is too light, the result usually is a slight loss of color intensity because of the thinner layer of ink deposited. Lighter pressure combined with an uneven surface of the paper at some locations can prevent the ink from adhering evenly to the paper surface. The result is random "skipping" of the design. This most often is seen as skipped sections along a thin, straight line.

Excessive inking or pressure produces a heavier deposit of ink on the paper. Color intensity is striking but subtlety in the design is lost as closely-spaced lines come close to merging.

The surface tension of the still-wet ink plus its thickness sometimes can combine with the lifting motion of the plates to produce minor smudging.

SPLATTERS

Splattering, a random spray of droplets of ink or oil, sometimes occurs during printing operations. Ink and oil splatters have different characteristics. Ink splatters usually do not exceed 1 mm. while oil soaks through the paper, resulting in larger spotting.

Splatters are a production defect which usually appear different from circulation-caused staining. Oil spotting is not common. Ink spottings rarely appear to have the same shade and thickness as the inks used to print, number, or sign the note. Close examination will make this difference obvious.

DISCOLORATION

Aging can cause the paper on which a note is printed to discolor. This is not a staining but a chemical reaction within the paper.
It is usually caused by exposure to oxygen in the air. Another cause for discoloration is the action of the chemical content of the paper (usually acid) as a result of the manufacturing process.

Discoloration does not necessarily occur uniformly across a note. It often occurs along an edge. High quality paper is less likely to show obvious discoloration, all things being equal.

FOXING

Foxing is a condition of long-term storage found on any old paper, not just old currency. It is noticed as small brownish-red spots which are in the paper itself, not just on the surface. The cause is an infestation of lice.

Severe foxing will result in the paper being pierced through the discolored spot.

Foxing is more common in older non-U.S. notes, although it can be found on a variety of currency issues of the United States.

ROUNDED CORNERS

Rounded corners often are the result of normal aging concentrating at the points of severest stress. Here, the cutting blade has trimmed fibers on two sides, causing some fibers to lose their secure anchorage. Aging will cause the corner to become frayed.

Handling also can produce frayed corners. This may appear no different from an aged corner.

Where the chemical processes associated with discoloration weaken fibers at the corners, some fibers may break off. This can be seen as a rounded corner with discoloration at that location. The corner also may become frayed.

INK MIGRATION

Ink migration applies to three conditions: printer's inking, serial number stamping, and hand writings. Over time, ink from any of these may travel through the paper and reach close enough to the opposing surface to be seen clearly. In extreme cases the ink may travel through the paper completely.

Ink migration usually occurs uniformly for each major element of the note's design. Each element (seal, border, vignette, etc.) may migrate at a different rate, however. Ink migration face-to-back often occurs at a different rate than that from back-to-face. This is due to differences in pigments and ink formulations used on the two sides.

Stamped serial numbers, as found on many Confederate States of America issues, often migrate at a non-uniform rate. The individual numbers of a stamping can migrate at different rates because the stamp was not uniformly inked or stamping pressure was not uniform.

Hand signed notes pose a different situation. The ink itself may migrate through the paper, as may any ink. However, differences in the amount of ink deposited and varying pen pressures can result in uneven migration. In addition, scratching of the paper surface by the nib of the pen can cause ink to move through the paper rapidly. If surface scratching by the pen is severe, the ink would flow immediately through the paper, causing an ink blot on the opposite side. If less severe, a discolored, blotchy appearance would result.

INK FADING

Ink fading can show itself in several ways. The color of inked areas of a note can lose intensity. A color can change from its original shade. Finally, in the case of hand-signed notes, the ink of the signature or other writings may actually lift off the surface of the note, leaving only a light ink residue.

Dark, well-inked areas will rarely lift off or lose intensity as a consequence of aging. Printer's ink contains high-quality binders and carbon pigments. These usually are quite effective at holding their integrity and intensity. Pastel colors are more prone to lose intensity as a result of exposure to air.

Pastels and bright colors in particular are prone to change shade. This results from chemical reaction to residues in the paper itself and to vapors and chemicals in the air.

Handwritten sections tend to be affected by aging more easily than printed sections because this ink usually lacks the binders and the intense pigmentation of printer's ink.

PERFORATIONS

Aging of paper tends to aggravate the defect known as a Thin Spot. Fibers in these weak areas tend to separate as they are flexed. With sufficient separation a hole begins to appear. These holes can occur even under careful handling by collectors. They normally are extremely small and difficult to detect unless held up to a strong light.

When the fibers break rather than separate the perforation resembles an irregular pinhole.

HOLES

United States notes of the nineteenth century occasionally are found with very small holes. The notes may otherwise appear uncirculated. The printers were often the cause. Some printers were known to pin or staple notes together with thin loops of wire, possibly for hanging to facilitate the drying process. It was also common for stacks of currency to be clipped together after they had been examined or counted. The result is one or two clear holes known as pinholes.

Once notes reached circulation, they were subject to a variety of conditions and situations which resulted in irregular holes of varying size. The edges of these holes are usually rough, with evidence of abrasion. They are most often found along folds in the note.

Merchants, in earlier times, were known to stack their notes on spindles, there being no cash registers available. These holes are significantly larger than pinholes.

TEARS

Tears occur as a result of normal circulation. Simple mishandling usually damages only the edge of a note. Less commonly, tears can extend well into the design. In extreme cases, a portion of a note may be torn completely off. Deliberate tears are indistinguishable from tears caused by mishandling or accidents.

The edges of tears are rough, with fibers often extending across the space between the edges of the tear.

If the cutting blade slips during note trimming, a nick can occur in the edge of a note. This actually is a Trimming Defect, distinguished from a tear by its smooth edges.

Separations of the paper along a fold are considered splits rather than tears.

CLIPPING

A clipped note has been trimmed so poorly that one or more edges pass through the design. It occurs during production at the time the notes are cut from the sheets.

This defect usually is quite light, barely touching the border framework. Less commonly, it reaches a bit deeper into the note.

High quality operations, such as those of the U.S. Bureau of Engraving and Printing or the American Bank Note Company, have rarely permitted clipped notes to pass into circulation. Still, these have occurred.

Low-quality printing operations are more likely to produce clipped notes. If these notes reach circulation it is most often a consequence of need rather than of a sloppy operation alone. For example, during the American Civil War the Confederate government had to contract with engravers and printers to produce their new currency. It had to be done quickly and in large volume with inadequate facilities and equipment. These notes usually were trimmed unevenly by hand. This led to the issuance of literally thousands of clipped notes. Thus, CSA notes can be found in superb condition yet with one or more edges clipped.

TRIM

Edge trim defects are produced at the time the notes are cut from sheets. An edge may not be cut perfectly straight or adjacent edges may not be at right angles to each other.

Misalignment of sheets in a cutting device or careless hand cutting can produce edges which are not at right angles to each other. Uneven trim, seen as an edge bowed smoothly or as an edge with several lightly-angled cuts, often occurs in notes trimmed by hand. A cutting blade which hesitates momentarily or which contains a nick can produce a jagged edge.

Trimming defects can happen both in high-quality and low-quality printing operations. Trimming defects are very common in Confederate States of America (CSA) notes, occuring even in notes which might otherwise be considered of GEM quality.

ROUGHNESS

Edge roughness can come from three sources: during trimming (a production defect), as a result of abrasion from handling, and breaking of the fibers at a fold. Sometimes these can be found in combination on the same note.

Abrasion is the most common cause of edge roughness. It often produces lengthy edge sections (typically more than 1 cm.) showing stray fibers. A slight dullness at these locations -- a bruised section with a loss of crispness -- is common. Minor soiling often
is found here.

An imperfection in the blade edge, or a very slight movement of the blade or paper during cutting can produce an edge with a section not cleanly and sharply cut. This can be seen as stray paper fibers protruding from the edge at one or more short sections (usually 1 mm. or less in length) along an otherwise smooth, crisp edge.

Constant folding at the same position can cause edge-fiber breakage at the fold line. A similar defect can result from a light bruising at a single sharp crease.

WEAR

Circulated notes eventually will show signs of wear. Rubbing is a common wearing action as notes are passed from hand to hand. Insertion and removal from billfolds and cash drawers will also produce surface wear.

Rubbing can cause actual displacement of surface fibers and/or destruction of these fibers. Ink placed on the paper by the commonly used intaglio process creates a raised surface, which is itself susceptible to wear.

The most obvious characteristic resulting from surface wear is a loss of detail at finely engraved lines. This wear rarely is uniform across the note. Thus, comparing different sections of the same note is an effective detection mechanism.

INK BREAK

Notes printed by the intaglio process are subject to breaks in the inked lines forming the raised image. This defect is found within a crease caused by repeated folding.

Similar-appearing defects are found in notes printed by other processes. However, since the inked design has penetrated the body of the paper rather than being primarily on its surface, there is no true ink break. The actual defect, upon close examination, is found to be fiber breakage. This is really the start of a split.

Minor ink breaks often are difficult to detect. They initially may be viewed as a clarity defect. The difference is that ink breaks will occur across many lines, tracing the path of the fold.

THIN SPOTS

The standards for modern currency paper are of the highest for any paper. Still, notes have been printed on lower-quality paper. Too, notes printed on paper with easily detected imperfections have been issued and circulated for many years.

Special currencies often are produced on paper of lower quality or on paper whose quality varies. Concentration Camp currency and private issues are typical examples. Wartime conditions can impair the issuing authority's ability to produce or acquire high quality paper. This was true of the Confederate States of America (CSA). Early paper making produced batches of varying quality. This can be seen in U.S. colonial issues.

A common quality defect in paper is a thin spot. This can be seen easily by holding the note to a strong light. The thin spot will transmit more light than the surrounding paper. The size can vary but typically is several millimeters in diameter. Thin spots are more likely to be affected by the aging processes.

SURFACE DEFECTS

There are two causes for surface defects found on paper currency. One cause is related to the colored threads often placed in currency papers. The other is related to the fibrous nature of paper.

Colored threads have long been added to currency papers to thwart counterfeiting. Early notes of the United States contained heavy threads. The thickness of these threads has caused two types of surface defects:

Sometimes a thread may lift from the paper surface and work loose. On an un-inked area this leaves a slight channel in the surface, usually barely noticeable and generally ignored. If the lifted thread comes from a printed area this produces the effect of missed inking. It is different from a Clarity Defect, for this Surface Defect can appear as a single un-inked line crossing several elements of the design.

If a thick thread lies solidly within the paper but extends partially above the surface of the note it may interfere with the proper depositing of ink at that location. The result of this surface defect is a mis-inking. It, too, looks different from a Clarity Defect since the thread usually is clearly outlined by the mis-inking.

Similar to the lifting of a thread is the pulling and removal of a mass of paper fibers from the surface of a note. This can occur either before or after printing. It is caused when a section of the paper surface sticks to the plate or roller as it lifts from the paper. It is a very uncommon defect in paper currency.

Lifted fibers create an irregularly-shaped depression in the surface, usually extremely shallow. If printing occurs over the area after the damage has been done the result may be almost undetectable. At most, a minor loss of sharpness in the design at that spot may occur if the ink soaks slightly into the damaged area.

If the surface is lifted after printing, a portion of the inked area is removed as well. This may leave a completely clear area. If the depression is extremely shallow, some ink may still be left in the damaged area. Without careful examination this may appear to be a clarity defect.

IMBEDDED MATTER

Paper is a fibrous material. During its manufacture, foreign matter may become mixed in with the raw materials before pressing and drying of the paper are completed. Also, some of the raw materials and chemicals may contain matter which does not separate or dissolve as intended. This unwanted matter can become trapped within the paper fibers.

The trapped matter can produce different effects on a note. It may merely be an off-colored spot in an otherwise clear area of the paper. It may offer a surface that does not accept inking the way the rest of the paper surface does, resulting in a mis-inking.

If the trapped matter is thicker than the rest of the paper or if it lifts from the paper's surface, it will produce a surface defect similar to that caused by a thread.

WRINKLES

Non-uniform drying and paper shrinkage, as well as imperfect papers, can produce crisp, uncirculated notes with extensive wrinkling. Such manufacturing and production defects are seen in some notes of the mid-nineteenth century U. S. southern states issues.

OTHER FACTORS AFFECTING GRADING

Certain types of notes may grade differently from what first appearances might normally indicate. The era, the location or circumstances of issuance, and the type of paper used are influencing factors. If a late 19th Century United States or British issue is taken as a standard reference, then notes printed on poorer-quality paper or under stressed conditions should be judged less critically. Special consideration might be accorded:

- Foxing and other aging, wrinkling, ink migration, skewed design, shifted design, abnormal margins:

    o Confederate States of America

- Colonial issues of North and South America
- Municipalities and other political subdivisions
- Older private issues

- Splatters, fading, roughly trimmed edges, clarity, surface defects, embedded matter:

  - Concentration Camp issues
  - German Notgeld
  - Colonial issues of North and South America
  - Confederate States of America
  - Municipalities and other political subdivisions
  - Older private issues

- Clipped edges:

  - Confederate States of America
  - United States Fractional Currency
  - Colonial issues of North and South America

Certain defects have become recognized as common for a particular issue. These are not arbitrary assignments at the whim of a collector or dealer. Proper grading requires that the collector or dealer be aware of the conditions surrounding the issuance of a particular type of note. Therefore, some review of similar notes, or catalog study and research, is warranted before the new collector can feel confident in negotiating a purchase or sale.

REFERENCES

The Standard Guide for Grading Paper Currency
    Irwin Tyler
    Ahl Kayn Publishers 2008

U.S. Essay, Proof and Specimen Notes
    Gene Hessler
    BNR Press, 1979

Guide to Detecting Altered & Counterfeit U.S. Coins & Currency
    Marc Hudgeons
    House of Collectibles, Inc., 1981

Standard Catalog of United States Paper Money
    Chester L. Krause and Robert F. Lemke
    Krause Publications, 1989

United States Postage & Fractional Currency 1862 - 1876
    Art Christoph and Chet Krause
    Numismatic News 1958

The Official 1982 Blackbook Price Guide of United States Paper Money
    Marc Hudgeons
    House of Collectibles, Inc., 1982

A Collector's Guide to Paper Money
    Yasha Beresiner
    Stein & Day 1977

The Comprehensive Catalog of U.S. Paper Money
    Gene Hessler
    BNR Press 1981

Collecting Paper Money - A Beginner's Guide
    Colin Narbeth
    Henry Regnery Company 1968

The Story of Paper Money
    Yasha Beresiner and Colin Narbeth
    Arco Publishing Company 1973

Paper Money of the United States
 Robert Friedberg
 The Coin and Currency Institute 1986

United States Large Size Paper Money 1861 to 1923
 William P. Donlon
 A.M. and Don Kagin, Inc. 1979

Many dealers' price lists

OTHER PUBLICATIONS BY IRWIN TYLER

Booklets:	Why Chiropractic?	2011
	Why Acupuncture?	2011
	Why Acupressure?	2012
	Why Homeopathy?	2012
	Grading Coins with Confidence	2012
Videos:	YouTube discussion on why Alternative Medicine often is a more effective approach than traditional medicine: **http://youtu.be/rD9B0v7GIFE**	
Books for Adults:	So Many Gates to the City…A Guide for the Modern Perplexed - A Book About Jewish Belief and Understanding, and Making Some Sense Of It	2008
	Targum Americana - The Bible Understood: Genesis - Bereishit	2013
	Points of Health - The Effectiveness and Safety of Acupuncture and Acupressure	2013
Books for Children:	The Special Piece of Chalah	2006
	The Chanukah I Remembered	2006

Printed in Great Britain
by Amazon